Excel for beginners

Learn Excel 2016, Including an Introduction to Formulas, Functions, Graphs, Charts, Macros, Modelling, Pivot Tables, Dashboards, Reports, Statistics, Excel Power Query, and More

© **Copyright 2018**

All rights Reserved. No part of this book may be reproduced in any form without permission in writing from the author. Reviewers may quote brief passages in reviews.

Disclaimer: No part of this publication may be reproduced or transmitted in any form or by any means, mechanical or electronic, including photocopying or recording, or by any information storage and retrieval system, or transmitted by email without permission in writing from the publisher.

While all attempts have been made to verify the information provided in this publication, neither the author nor the publisher assumes any responsibility for errors, omissions or contrary interpretations of the subject matter herein.

This book is for entertainment purposes only. The views expressed are those of the author alone, and should not be taken as expert instruction or commands. The reader is responsible for his or her own actions.

Adherence to all applicable laws and regulations, including international, federal, state and local laws governing professional licensing, business practices, advertising and all other aspects of doing business in the US, Canada, UK or any other jurisdiction is the sole responsibility of the purchaser or reader.

Neither the author nor the publisher assumes any responsibility or liability whatsoever on behalf of the purchaser or reader of these materials. Any perceived slight of any individual or organization is purely unintentional.

Contents

INTRODUCTION 1
CHAPTER 1: BASICS 3
CHAPTER 2: FORMULAS 19
CHAPTER 3: FUNCTIONS 24
CHAPTER 4: MACROS 34
CHAPTER 5: VERTICAL AND HORIZONTAL LOOKUP 40
CHAPTER 6: PIVOT TABLES 44
CHAPTER 7: DATA MODELS 51
CHAPTER 8: POWER VIEW 58
CHAPTER 9: VBA BASICS 61
CONCLUSION 68

Introduction

Microsoft Excel is an extremely useful and malleable program that is also rather 'bareboned' when it comes to presenting you with all of your available options. When you are first starting out, it is important to remember that using Excel is a skill, and as with any skill, it can be improved over time. So don't get discouraged; it will get easier each day you use it.

If you know how to use it properly, Excel can provide you with all of the tools needed to organize a wide variety of information types in a grid-based interface. Excel has been around for nearly thirty years, and many of the features offered in the first edition of the software are still going strong today.

One of the primary uses for Excel comes from the financial sector as Excel allows users to create their own formulas and use them to calculate anything from as complex as a corporation's annual report all the way down to a simple sales forecast. You will also find Excel used for a variety of organizational and tracking tasks including invoicing, contact lists, status reports and more. The program is also useful when it comes to working with large sets of data, such as during statistical analysis for its graphing and charting functions.

Excel stores data in workbooks and each workbook can contain as many worksheets as you need. Worksheets are individual and fully customizable spreadsheets which you will interact with directly. Worksheets are broken down into horizontal rows and vertical columns with each row and column broken down into individual cells. Interacting with cells is the primary form of interaction when it comes to worksheets and cells can store text as well as numbers.

If filled with numbers, each cell can also be linked to other cells through the use of mathematical formulas. Cells can be told to use formulas and then display the results of the calculation. Each cell can also be given a unique color, border, font and more. When using Excel, you can create formulas or make use of a wide variety of formulas already preprogrammed. The preprogrammed formulas offer a wide variety of options including calculating interest payments, determining the standard deviation, and most common mathematical and financial equations.

While you are most likely familiar with the table function found in Microsoft Word, the charts available in Excel offer a much wider range of visualization options from a simple pie chart to complicated multipoint pivot charts. When it comes to complicated formatting and sorting of lots of data, Excel tends to be your best choice, especially if the graphed data may need to change on the fly.

The other main thing that Excel does extremely well is helping to identify trends by making specific variables much easier to view in chart form. The wide variety of variables at your fingertips makes understanding complex ideas much easier and less time-consuming. This is in part because of the way that you can use Excel to bring disparate points of data together through the use of workbooks and interconnected worksheets. What it boils down to is that if you are in an information-based field and you are not yet using Excel or an analog regularly, you are most likely putting in more work than you need to in order to achieve the results you want.

Chapter 1: Basics

Entering and Editing Data

If you wish to enter text or numbers

• Choose the cell you wish to fill with your data and designate your choice by clicking on it.

• Enter the information you would like to put into the cell and finish by pressing either the TAB key or the ENTER key. If you instead wish to move to a new line in the already existing cell, instead press the ENTER key in conjunction with the ALT key.

If you wish to enter data into multiple cells at once

• Begin by selecting the cell or cells you wish to include the data.

• If you wish to select only one cell, you simply click on it, but if you wish to select multiple cells, you instead click on the first one in the series and then hold down the mouse button and drag your mouse to the final cell in the series.

12	1	7/9/2018	$5,000.00	$425.75	$100.00
13	2	8/9/2018	$4,490.92	$425.75	$100.00
14	3	9/9/2018	$3,980.14	$425.75	$100.00
15	4	10/9/2018	$3,467.65	$425.75	$100.00
16	5	11/9/2018	$2,953.46	$425.75	$100.00
17	6	12/9/2018	$2,437.56	$425.75	$100.00
18	7	1/9/2019	$1,919.94	$425.75	$100.00
19	8	2/9/2019	$1,400.59	$425.75	$100.00
20	9	3/9/2019	$879.50	$425.75	$100.00

• If you wish to select quite a few cells at once, you may simply click on the first cell you wish to select while at the same time holding down the SHIFT key until you click on the final cell that you wish to be selected, as long as you are holding down the SHIFT key you can scroll to ensure you select the right cell.

- If you wish to select all of the cells on the current sheet, you simply press the button between the list of horizontal and vertical cell names or press the CTRL key in conjunction with the A key.
- If you wish to select a group of cells that are not close to one another, simply select the first cell and then hold down the CTRL key by selecting the other cells. This can also be achieved by holding down the SHIFT key in conjunction with the F8 key; this will allow you to select cells without having to hold down any keys.
- If you wish you select an entire column or row, simply click on the heading for that column or row.
- After you have selected the cells you wish to contain the duplicate date, type the information into the cell and then press the CTRL key and the ENTER key in conjunction with one another.

If you wish to move data from one cell to another

- Begin by selecting the cell or group of cells whose data you wish to copy.
- Find the clipboard group, located in the home tab. Here, you will find the cut and copy options. Pressing the CTRL key in conjunction with the Z key will cut and copy the selected text at the same time.
- Copy and cut can be done separately from the keyboard as well. You start by pressing the CTRL key in conjunction with the C key for copy and the X key for cut.
- Now select the new home for the data and clip paste in the clipboard area or press the CTRL key and the V key.
- Pasting new data into a cell overwrites the data already in that cell. If you wish to prevent that, click the arrow located beneath the paste option, click paste special and select the relevant option.
- Selecting a cell and then right-clicking on it will also provide these options.
- This will work for cells, rows, and columns in the say way.
- From the paste option in the clipboard group, you can also copy formulas, formatting or values from one cell to another by selecting the appropriate option.

If you wish to fill a cell with a time or a date

• Begin by choosing the cell you wish to fill with data.

• If you wish to include a specific date, enter the number as either 1/1/91 or 1-Jan-1991.

• When you enter a time in the afternoon or evening, it is important to write it as 8:00 pm as Excel will list a time as A.M. by default.

• If you wish to enter the current time and date, simply press the CTRL key, the SHIFT key and the semicolon key in conjunction with one another.

• If you wish to set a cell to always display the current time and date, you can type NOW or TODAY respectively.

• To ensure that the time or date listed uses the default format assigned to your computer in the Regional and Languages options menu, simply press the CTRL key, the SHIFT key and the @ key in conjunction with one another.

If you wish to set a set of cells to modify all numbers in a fixed way

• Find the Microsoft Office button in the top left corner and click on it.

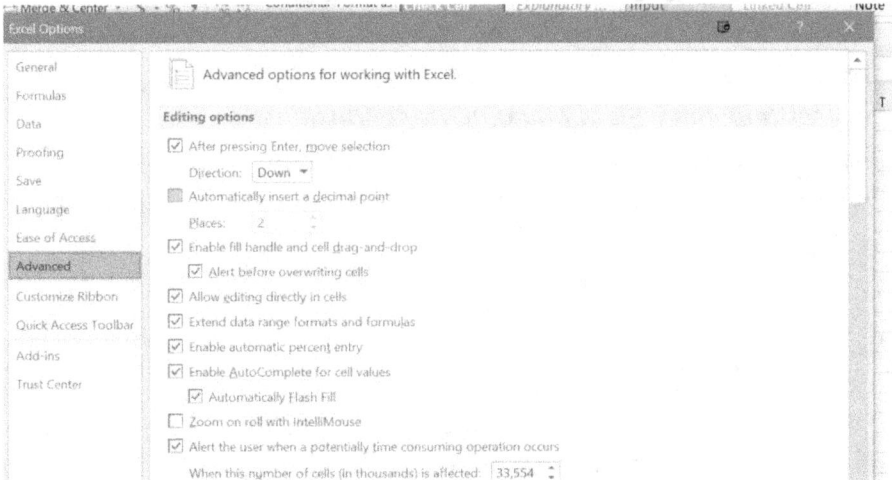

• Choose the advanced option, then editing options insert decimal point automatically.

- Now find the box listed as places and enter a positive number to make a decimal or a negative number to increase the resulting number.
- For example, entering 2 in the box before typing 182 into a cell, would result in the number 1.82.

If you wish to enter a sequence of numbers
- Begin by placing the first number into a cell.
- Place the second number of the pattern into the next cell in the column.
- Select the first two cells then click on the bottom right corner of the selected columns, also known as the fill handle, and drag to encompass the cells you wish to fill.
- Release the left mouse button.

If you wish to enter formulas and functions
- Choose a cell where you wish to enter the data and select it before finding the function bar which is the bar above the row names.
- In the function bar, begin entering your formula by starting with the = sign.
- Next fill in the cells you wish to include in the formula, for example, A1+A2. You will now see that Excel has calculated the value of A1+A2 in the cell you selected.

If you wish to enter SUM and other functions quickly
- Pressing the CTRL key in conjunction with the Shift key and the " key will copy the value from the preceding cell into the formula bar.

15	4	10/9/2018	$3,422.75	$425.75	$100.00
16	=IF([@[PMT NO]]<>"",ScheduledPayment,"")=IF([@[PMT				$100.00
17	NO]]<>"",ScheduledPayment,"")=IF([@[PMT NO]]<>"",				$100.00
18	ScheduledPayment,"")=IF([@[PMT NO]]<>"",				$100.00
19	ScheduledPayment,"")=IF([@[PMT NO]]<>"",				$100.00
20	ScheduledPayment,"")=IF([@[PMT NO]]<>"",				$100.00
21	ScheduledPayment,"")=IF([@[PMT NO]]<>"",				$0.00

- Pressing the CTRL key in conjunction with the ' key will show you the formulas at play in all of your cells.
- Pressing the Shift key in conjunction with the F3 key will display the insert function box and a number of function options.

- Pressing the Shift key in conjunction with the F9 key will calculate everything in the current worksheet.
- Typing =SUM(and then a list of cells closed with parentheses will add all of the cells listed.
- Including another number after the list of cells will find the sum of the cells before adding the additional number.

If you wish to switch between absolute and relative cell references
- Begin by choosing the cell which has the formula you are interested in switching between relative and absolute.
- Relative references are the default, which means cells results will change as they move around the worksheet.
- To change this, select the formula that is displayed in the formula bar and press F4 to switch between the two types.

Manipulating Cells

If you wish to adjust various settings
- If you wish to change how the ENTER key affects your work, you can set it to move to the next cell in a variety of directions.
- This can be found by selecting Excel Options, Advanced, Edit, Enter Move Selection.
- If you wish to change how wide a column is, begin by selecting the column you wish to change before looking for the format option under cells on the home tab.
- The size option will allow you to either set the column width to be auto-determined by the information contained within or set it to a specific width.

If you wish to display more information in a cell at one time
- This is referred to as wrapping text. To begin, choose the cell that contains the text you wish to wrap.
- From there, find the alignment option which can be found on the home tab.
- If the text is one long stream, you should widen the column or make the text smaller to ensure you can read all of it.

- If the text wraps, but you still can't read all of it, you need to format the row cell size by finding the AutoFit row option under the Format and cell size options on the home tab.

If you wish to create a drop-down list
- Begin by choosing the worksheet you wish to add the list to.
- Add the information you wish to appear as a list in connected cells either as a row or in a column.
- If you wish to sort the data alphabetically or numerically, select all of the data, before finding the data tab at the top of the screen and choosing the sort and filter option.
- After you have sorted your data, the next step is to select all of the cells you wish to include in the drop-down list before right-clicking and selecting the define name option.
- From there it is simply a matter of assigning a name to the list and clicking OK. It is important that the name be one word with no spaces.
- Choose a new cell in a worksheet that you wish to link to the drop-down data before choosing the data validation button.
- Under setting, select allow list, then in the box labeled "source", type the equal sign followed by the name of your list before checking the box labeled "in cell dropdown", and click OK.

If you wish to insert columns and cells
- Begin by selecting the cell where you wish to add additional cells – if you wish to add seven more cells then you would first have to select seven cells.
- Find the cells group on the home tab, choose to insert, then insert cells. This can also be achieved by selecting a group of cells, right-clicking and selecting insert cells.
- Determine the specifics as asked.
- If you wish to repeat the same duplication multiple times, press the CTRL key and the Y key in conjunction with one another.
- If you wish to alter the formatting options that are copied to the new cell, choose the insert options choice from the insert tab.

- To add additional rows or columns, select a complete row or column then find the insert tab and choose either insert a row or insert a column.

If you wish to delete rows, cells or columns
- Begin by selecting the row, cell or column that you have determined needs deletion.
- Find the cells group in the home tab and select the delete option.
- Right-clicking on the selected portion of text will also provide you with a delete option.
- Determine how you want the remaining cells to realign.
- If you wish to delete a large amount of content select the content and press the CTRL key in conjunction with the Y key.
- If you wish to return a portion of cut content to the worksheet, then press the CTRL key in conjunction with the Z key. This will only work if you haven't added any new information since you deleted what you want to save.

Manipulating Worksheets

If you wish to rename a worksheet
- Find the bar at the bottom of your current worksheet that shows the tabs for each open worksheet.
- Right-click on the sheet you wish to change the name of and then select rename.
- If you wish to make it so your sheet names are visible when the worksheet is printed, go to the insert tab and select the Header/Footer option.
- Find the sheet name option and insert the name of the sheet.

If you wish to move a worksheet

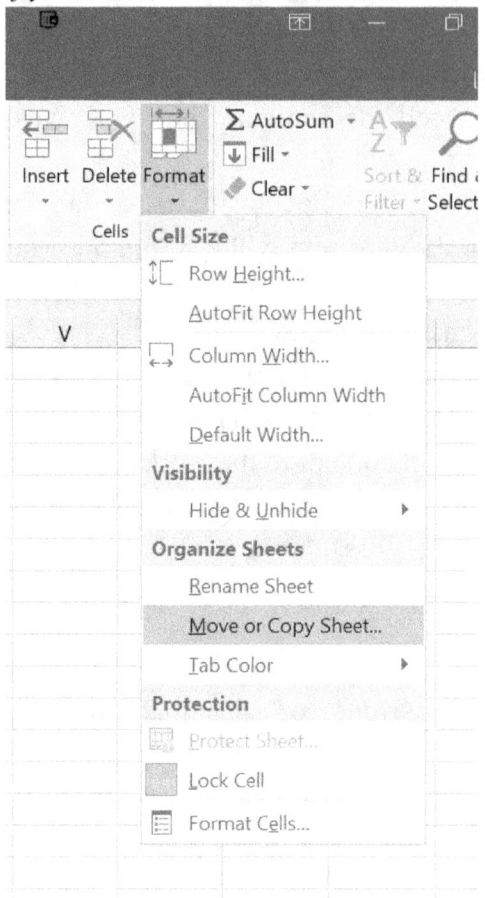

• To move a single worksheet, begin by selecting the sheet from the sheet tab, the arrow buttons will allow you to move between available sheets.

• If you want to move multiple sheets, select the first one, press the SHIFT key and hold it down, then select the other sheet you wish to move.

• If you wish to select sheets that are not near one another, simply replace the SHIFT key with the CTRL key when selecting sheets.

• If you wish to move all of the worksheets in a workbook, instead right-click on the sheet bar and select the select all sheets option.

- Once you have selected the sheets you are interested in moving to, find the cells group on the home tab.
- Choose the format option followed by organize sheets, then move the sheet.
- You will now see a list of options regarding where the sheet should be moved; selecting a sheet will place the moved sheet after the selected sheet.
- The move to end option will place the moved sheet at the end of the selected workbook; workbooks need to be opened in order to accept new pages.
- If you are just interested in moving a sheet around in the current notebook, instead simply click on it in the sheet bar and drag it to its new location.

If you wish to copy a worksheet

- Once you have selected the sheets you are interested in moving, find the cells group on the home tab.
- Choose the format option followed by organize sheets, then copy sheet.
- You will now see a list of options regarding where the sheet should be copied; selecting a sheet will place the copied sheet after the selected sheet.
- Right-clicking on the sheet in the sheet tab will also present these options.
- To copy sheets between workbooks, it is important to ensure both workbooks are open before proceeding.
- To just copy data between worksheets, select the data you wish to copy, press the CTRL key in conjunction with the C key, and then select the worksheet you wish to place the data into, and press the CTRL key in conjunction with the V key.

If you wish to insert a new worksheet

- Select the worksheet you wish to proceed the new worksheet and find the + button on the sheet tab row.
- If you instead wish to insert the new worksheet in front of the existing worksheet, find the cells group on the home tab.

- Choose to insert, then insert a new sheet.
- This can also be accomplished by right-clicking on a tab then choosing the insert option from the general tab.
- To add multiple worksheets at once, hold down the SHIFT key while selecting tabs from the sheet tab row.
- Once you have selected how many tabs you would like to create, right-click and select insert, then insert a worksheet.
- A number of new sheets equal to the number of sheets you selected will be created.

If you wish to delete a worksheet
- Select the worksheet or worksheet in question using the sheet tab.
- Find the cells group in the home tab before finding the delete option and clicking the arrow to reveal more options.
- Chose the delete sheet option.
- Finding the sheet you wish to delete in the sheet row tab, and right-clicking on it, will also reveal an option to delete.

If you wish to edit multiple worksheets simultaneously
- If you select multiple worksheets at the same time, using the worksheet row tab, then you are presented with several options, including to change multiple tab colors at once and to view their formulas and functions.

If you wish to enter data across multiple worksheets
- Begin by clicking on the tab of the first worksheet you wish to input data into; the tab should be visible near the top of the screen.
- Click on the first tab, then drag to include the breadth of the tabs you wish to add data to.
- Select the group of cells you wish to add data to before selecting the first one and adding the required data.
- At this point, pressing either the TAB key or the ENTER key will copy the data into the next selected cell.
- Repeat until you have achieved the desired results.

Formatting

If you wish to format number cells

• Click on the cells you wish to add number formatting to so they are selected.

• Press the CTRL key in conjunction with the 1 key to bring up the format cells box.

• This box lists a variety of ways that numbers can be formatted. These include: fractions, percentages, units of time, date, a wide variety of currencies, and more.

• Many of these categories have additional formatting options as well – if you need to make use of them, be sure to view all of the various available options.

• These options can also be accessed from the cells grouping on the home tab by choosing the format and then format cells all the way at the bottom.

If you wish to clear cells of their formatting

• Click on the cells you wish to remove formatting from so they are selected.

• Find the editing grouping under the home tab and choose the clear option.

• Selecting the additional options arrow will allow you to remove formatting as well as several other options.

If you wish to add borders, shading or text color to cells

• Click on the cells you wish to add formatting to so they are selected.

• Press the CTRL key in conjunction with the 1 key to bring up the format cells box.

• This box lists a variety of ways you can change the formatting, including the alignment, the border, the font, and the background color of the cells.

• Many of these categories have additional formatting options as well – if you need to make use of them, be sure to view all of the various available options.

- These options can also be accessed from the cells grouping on the home tab by choosing the format, and then format cells all the way at the bottom.

If you wish to use page break preview to adjust page breaks
- To view the page breaks as they are currently assigned, begin by opening the print options dialogue by choosing to print from the file menu or pressing the CTRL key in addition to the P key.
- You should now see all of the page breaks in your worksheet.
- This can also be accomplished by clicking on the view tab and choosing page break preview.
- To make a new break in the page, select the row or column you want the break to follow and then select the breaks icon and choose insert page break.
- To move page breaks by simply dragging them, choose the file tab, then options, then editing options then advanced.
- Ensure the box marked cell drag/drop is checked before clicking OK.
- Now when you are on the page break preview page, you should be able to modify page breaks just by clicking and dragging them.

Printing

If you wish to preview your worksheet prior to printing
- Begin by selecting the worksheet(s) you wish to view before printing.
- Choose file, then print, and a preview of your worksheets will appear.
- Pressing the CTRL key in conjunction with F2 will also bring up a print preview.
- Here you will be able to show your margins and also make changes to your pages, including alternating margins in addition to both headers and footers.
- The sheet options also give you the option of repeating rows or columns, adding gridlines, showing row/column headings, showing comments, showing cell errors, and manipulating page order.

If you wish to scale what you are printing

- If you wish to make what you are printing larger, smaller, or ensure that it fits to a single page, you begin by going to the page layout tab in the worksheet you wish to alter.
- From there, find the page setup options and click the button next to page setup.
- Find the page tab, then the scaling option.
- If you wish to alter how many pages tall or wide a worksheet is, find the "fit to" boxes on the scaling tab; the first box is the width, the second is the height.
- Setting either box to 1 will ensure the entire worksheet fits on one sheet either wide or tall.
- If you wish to fit your worksheet on a set number of pages just enter that number into the "fit to" boxes; however, any page breaks you added manually will not be included if "fit to" has been chosen.

If you wish to print to a specific area

- Find the page setup options and click the button next to page setup in the worksheet you wish to print a portion of.
- Find the page layout tab, then choose print area followed by set print area; be careful when setting this option as it will remain with the worksheet until you change it.
- Set the area you wish to print – if you select groupings of cells that are not close to one another, each grouping will print on its own page.

Name Box

Excel also gives you the ability to name cells and groups of cells to ensure that you can easily reference them quickly at a later point and time. Defined names can also be added to specific values and formulas to ensure that the user will always be able to tell what specific parts of a given workbook pertain to. A range of cells does not have to be connected to be part of the same name either. Once it has been defined, a name can even be used with additional cells or rages as a type of shorthand. Names can also overlap on specific cells. If this is the case, then both names will be displayed if the cell is selected.

Initially, you may not see the benefit in naming ranges of cells, however, after you start using them regularly, you will see their usefulness. Reasons to try defined names include things like how range names are far simpler to remember as they provide context to the data that makes it easier to come back to after prolonged absences. Additionally, ranges with names are automatically saved for extremely easy navigation. To view your currently named items, you can use the Edit tab, followed by the Goto option, before then selecting the name box. You can also use the find function as a means of finding any range that has a name in the current notebook.

Furthermore, ranges with names can be easily changed, and the change is automatically updated across all references of the name in question, be it in conditional formatting scenarios, calls for validation and even in various pivot tables or charts – essentially pretty much anywhere where accessing the reference would otherwise become both complicated and time-consuming. Generally speaking, ranges with names are always going to be easier to remove from various references or otherwise edit than non-named ranges. Ranges with names are also typically saved in such a way that they can be edited, replaced or removed without having to manually fix each reference to the range if anything changes.

Name rules

When it comes to naming individual cells, the conventions for doing so are quite precise. For starters, the first character of the name needs to be either an underscore, letter or backslash. The letters/characters C, c, R, and r cannot be used because they are primarily used as shorthand for rows and columns. The rest of the characters in the name can be made up of the same characters as well as numbers and periods as well. Regardless of the name, however, if the name is defined, then it can't also be a direct cell reference. Each defined name can include as many as 255 individual characters, but spaces are not allowed. No name is case specific.

Scope of defined names

A given defined name can be either a single worksheet or an entire workbook. The scope of a given defined name can be seen from the start based on the way in which the name is written, which is also the way in which Excel will know to find it – if you have a separate worksheet open at the same time you are searching for it.

- Simple names like Example_01 are automatically considered to be worksheet exclusive.

- To ensure a defined name applies to all of the workbooks of which it is a part, you will need to add a prefix. For example, with Sheet#!Example_01, the sheet# is equal to the current worksheet number. Meanwhile, the defined name must then be separated using an exclamation point.

Using the name box to create a range

You can create individual ranges with specific names in many different ways. The first involves the name box which is next to the formula box.

- To begin, you will need to choose the range or cell you wish to name before then selecting the name box and adding in the new name. You confirm the changes you made using the ENTER key. If the name contains any invalid information, then it will not be saved.

While the name box is easy to use, it is not without its flaws, starting with the fact that you cannot use it to create duplicate names, even if the things that are being named are not in the same worksheet. Additionally, names cannot then be edited using the name box, and the name box also will not show the full scope of the range of a given name. Finally, it is really only good for creating defined names within the worksheet you are currently working with.

Automatically create defined names

To create a defined name, you will first want to select the option to Create Names from the Selection in the Name Manager set of options within the Formulas tab. If you plan on creating numerous names, then you will want to start using it as soon as you start the new workbook and then stick with it as things are likely to get confusing if you mix and match.

Keep the following in mind when using this option to achieve the best results:

• Always label your rows and columns in the same way to ensure that you will be able to easily recognize them when the new defined names are added. Spaces will always be replaced with underscores.

• Defined names will only ever refer to the cells which contain data, not the column or row labels.

• All the defined names created in this way will be workbook specific.

Chapter 2: Formulas

Generally speaking, you can count on Excel to have a number of conditional rules in place to ensure that things are formatted correctly. If that doesn't seem as though it will be enough to meet your needs, then you will instead need to use formulas to ensure everything is just right. Excel formulas also have the ability to be conditional which means you can create formulas that are only active when certain conditions are met via the AND, IF and OR commands.

The steps you will find in this chapter have replaced the Conditional Sum Wizard of previous versions. While this add-on is not available any longer, if you come across old formulas that were created using it, then you can still get them to work by placing them in the formula bar. You can also place them into a cell directly by first choosing the cell and then selecting the option for Formulas. From there you will want to choose Add a Function before pasting the results into the Function Arguments box.

Conditional formulas formatting basics

• Start by selecting the group of cells or single cell that you wish to format.
• Choose the Home tab before selecting the option for Conditional Formatting and then choose the option for New Rule when it becomes available.

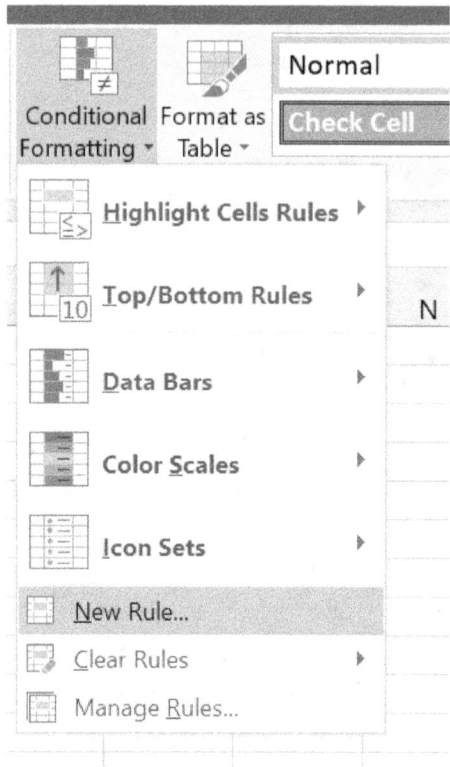

- From there, choose the option that lets you select the cells to be formatted.
- Choose the cell which you wish to place the formula in or format based on an existing formula. Often copy and pasting is the easiest way to do so.
- Select the formatting option and then choose the formatting specifics that you want to change based on the existing formula.
- Don't forget to hit OK in order to accept your choices. If everything was done properly, then you should see the results reflected in the selected cells.

Conditional formula examples

- To point out cells which are currently blank: select the cells you want to check, follow the steps above, and then enter this formula =Cell1="" where Cell1 is the first cell you wish to check.

- To point out cells which contain the same values: follow the steps above and then enter this formula =COUNTIF($A$1:$D$11,D2)>1.
- To find the average of a set of cells: start by choosing which cell will contain the answer before entering this formula =Cell1>AVERAGE(Cell1:Cell2) where Cell1 is the first cell in the list and Cell2 is the last cell in the list.
- To find all of the values that meet multiple specific conditions enter =AND (the specifics you are looking for). Cells which meet the conditions will say true; the rest will read false.
- To find a list of values that meet one of a variety of conditions enter =OR(the specifics you are looking for). Cells which meet at least one of the conditions will say true; the rest will read false.
- To change what phrase the cells list into something besides true and false enter =IF(AND(your specifications), "Phrase1,"Phrase2") where phrase 1 and phrase 2 are what you wish to replace true and false with.
- To add a variety of tiered grades based on values in certain cells, select the cells you wish to grade, then
enter=IF(cell1>number1,"grade1"IF(cell1>number2, "grade2" etc.
In this case, cell1 is the first cell in the list, number 1 is the first tier of grading, and grade 1 is what will be displayed as a result.

Duplicate existing conditional formatting or formulas

- To duplicate an existing conditional format or formula into a new worksheet, the first thing you will need to do is select the cell with the formatting you plan on copying.
- From there, you will want to seek out the Format Painter option that can be found underneath the Home tab. When selected correctly, it will turn your mouse icon into a paintbrush icon.
- With this accomplished, you will then simply need to drag the paintbrush to the group of cells that you want to apply the formatting or formula to. When done correctly, this should cause all of the formatting to transfer over directly, and it will save you from having to update any specific references in the formula manually.

• If the references do not update automatically, then you will have to do so manually, which you can do by selecting the cell which contains the new version of the formula.

• You will then want to choose the references you want to change before pressing F4 to see how the reference is seen by the spreadsheet.

• Cell references are then set to relative by default which means that each cell is going to read the reference in relation to the location it currently finds itself in. If the reference is an absolute reference, however, then the cells listed are used as part of the formula regardless of where the formula might find itself.

• When you are done with the paintbrush icon, you can banish it by hitting the ESC key. If you want to use it to paint another set of cells with the same information, then you just need to double-click on the Format Painter option.

Removing conditional formatting

If you wish to remove conditional formatting or formulas from a set of cells or a specific cell, then you will start by selecting the cells with the formatting that you want to remove.

• From there you will want to choose the Home tab and then choose the Conditional Formatting option.

• Next, you will want to select the option for Data Validation, followed by the box labeled Same.

• Next, choose the option that will allow you to clear the rules as well as the option to clear the rules from the selected cells.

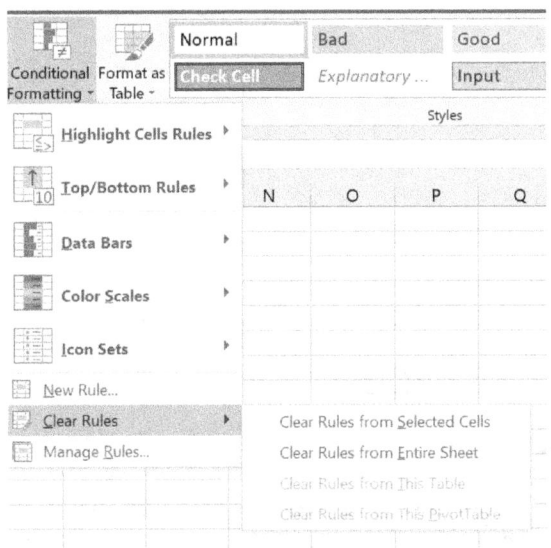

- To clear all of the worksheet's formatting, select the Clear Rules option from the Conditional Formatting tab and finally choose the option to remove formatting from the full worksheet if that is what you wish to do.

Chapter 3: Functions

Data Validation Functions

Data validation functions are a useful Excel feature that can give you the ability to generate a list of specific entries that can then limit the values that can be successfully placed in a given cell. It also allows you to create messages that inform the user of the types of data that can be put into the cells. You can also include automatic warnings if the wrong data is entered and even find any instances of wrong information thanks to the handy Audit function. You can even determine a range of specific values to be placed in a cell or determine the range based on the results of a predetermined cell.

Set what can be entered into a cell

To ensure that only a set list of values can be placed into a given cell, or that a cell will only accept certain numbers, the first thing you need to do is to set a list of acceptable values before setting the cell to know what's what.

- To start, you will want to select the A1 cell by clicking on it.
- With that done, you will then want to locate the Data menu, and then the option labeled Validation.
- From there, you want to choose the Settings option before then choosing the List option from the resulting drop-down menu.

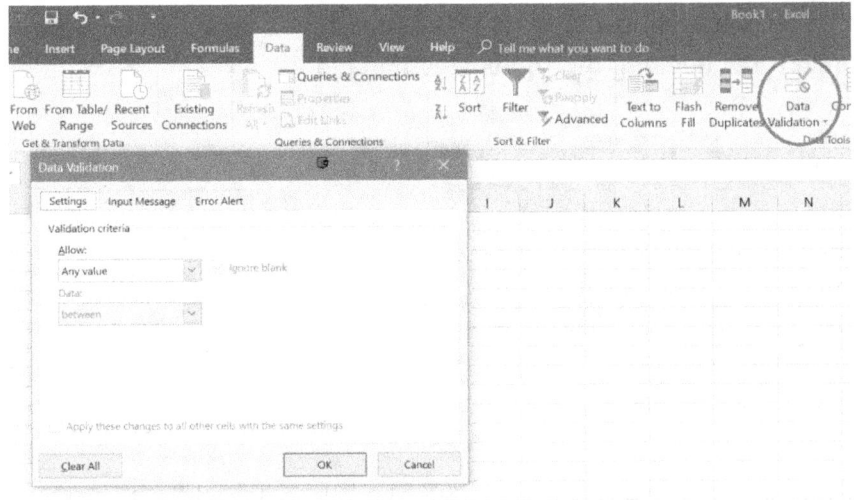

- From the resulting menu, you will want to locate the option labeled Source and fill the relevant box with a,b,c and then confirm your actions. If you prefer, you can instead fill this box with a specific cell reference or a named range. If you go one of these routes, you will need to include an equal sign (=) before listing the specifics.
- Assuming you have done everything correctly up until this point you should now see in A1 a list that provides all of the values that can be used within. Selecting one of the options will then ensure it appears in the cell. You can also type values into the cell, though only those that are allowed will remain when you click off of it.

List what data is allowed

Once you have created a message, you will see it each time you select a cell that has limited input options. You will be able to move the location of the message at will or determine if it shows up in an active Office Assistant.

- You will begin by choosing the cell that you want to place the message in. You will still need to choose a starter cell even if you plan for the message to ultimately show up within an active Office Assistant.

- Next, you will select the Data menu and then select the Validation option before choosing the Input Message tab.

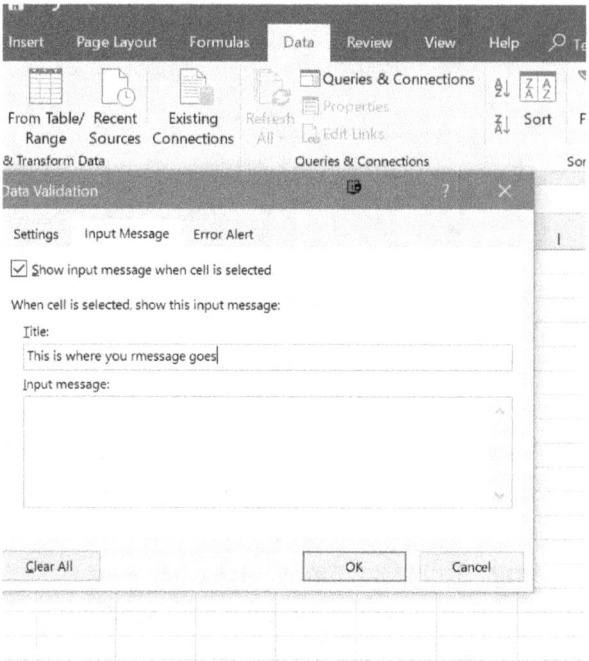

- Make sure that the option that indicates if the message is going to be shown is checked before selecting the Title box and adding in the title of your message. Finally, enter the message that you want to send into the box labeled Message and be sure to click OK when leaving this page; otherwise, nothing will be saved.

Enter a "wrong data entered" message

This type of message can manifest itself in a few different ways. First, they can prevent the wrong data from being entered in the first place and second, they can only tell the user when an error has occurred. It is also possible to simply limit the data that can be added to a cell without providing any clarification as to why that might be the case.

- Choose the cell you wish to add the message to.

- Select the menu labeled Data before selecting the option labeled Validation and choosing the tab labeled Error Alert.
- Ensure the show alert box is checked before determining the type of message you want to set.
- If you want to create the type of message that won't allow the wrong values to be added to a cell, choose the list labeled Style and select the Stop option. Add a title for the message in the box labeled Title and the bulk of the message in the box labeled Message. The message should list what values are allowed. Ensure you click OK, or nothing will be saved.
- If you want to create a message that will warn the user of incorrect values, instead visit the Style list and choose the Warning option. This will force the user to choose to continue when incorrect values are added to specific cells. Add a title for the message in the box labeled Title and the bulk of the message in the box labeled Message. The message should list what values are allowed. Ensure you click OK, or nothing will be saved.
- If you want to create a message that will simply inform the user of incorrect values, instead visit the Style list and choose the Inform option. Add a title for the message in the box labeled Title and the bulk of the message in the box labeled Message. The message should list what values are allowed. Ensure you click OK, or nothing will be saved.

Using the Audit toolbar

Once you have made it clear to the system what limits exist on the type of data that can be added to a cell, you can then double check that all of the existing information is within the boundaries of what's acceptable. Incorrect cells will be highlighted for ease of use.

- First, you will want to select the Tools menu before locating and selecting the Customize option.
- From the resulting choices, you will need to select Toolbars from the dialog window that appears before then ensuring the box for Auditing is checked.

- Once you close that window, you will then want to locate the Auditing toolbar and choose the option for highlighting invalid data. You will then find that if you fix the error, the issue is removed from the list.

Determine the range of acceptable values

You are free to set specific maximums and minimums for values that are allowed within a specific cell. This will also make it possible for you to determine if the cell you are working on at the moment will affect other cells as a result of your actions.

- To start, you will need to choose the cell you want to add the limits to.
- Next, find the Data menu and choose the option for Validation before selecting the Setting stab.

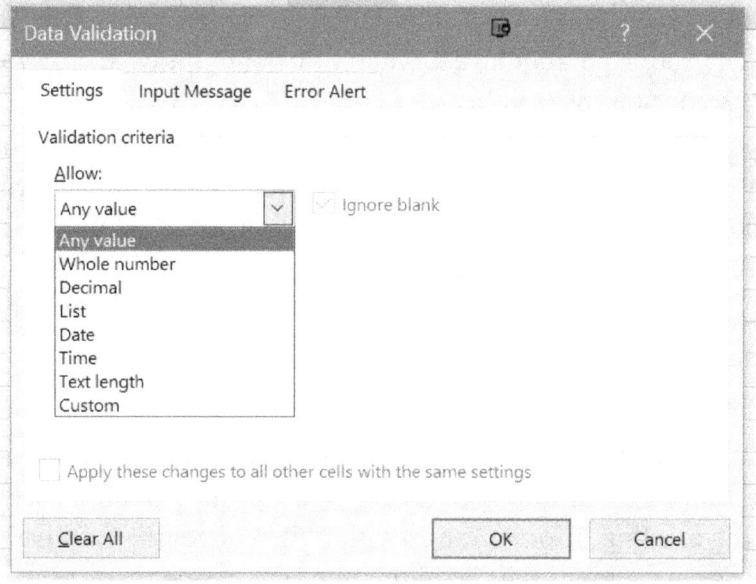

- From there, you will want to choose the list for Allow and then choose the option to Allow whole numbers. You will then select the Data option and then choose the option for Between from the resulting list.
- Finally, you will need to enter both a maximum and a minimum number, or you could use a set cell reference depending on what you

need the worksheet for. All that is left to do is to click OK and ensure all the specifics are saved successfully.

Ensure a cell is valid based on its relationship to another cell

If need be, you can also ensure that cells will only allow certain values to be entered based on their relationship with other cells.

• To start, you will want to choose the Data menu, then locate the option for Validation, followed by the Settings tab.

• Next, you will select the Allow list, followed by the option to Customize.

• Choose the box labeled Formula and then enter this formula: IF(cell1>cell2, TRUE, FALSE) and then simply replace Cell1 and Cell2 with the specific cells that you are looking to connect to one another. You can also use other functions besides IF, though it needs to always include the true and false option and don't forget the equals sign.

• Ensure your function is saved by hitting OK, and you are good to go.

Matrixial Functions

Matrices can be calculated using Excel in numerous ways: the MMULT function is useful in determining the results of multiplying two arrays which are used as stand-ins for matrices; the MUNIT function is used to determine the matrix of a unit when given a specific dimensional reference; the MDETERM function is used to determine the measure of scale for a square matrix; and the MINVERSE function is used to determine the inverse of a matrix square.

MMULT

When formatting this function, you will want to write it as MMULT (array1, array2) in which each array is a group of values that are spread throughout any number of predetermined cells that, if taken together, represent two connected matrices. As such, each array needs to be written as Cell1:Cell2 with Cell1 containing the first matrix cell details and the second cell containing the second matrix details. These arrays can successfully be written as both constants and references. If you are using Excel Online, then you will not be able to take advantage of array formulas.

To ensure you correctly produce an array result for the function once you enter it into the function bar, it is critical that you first press the CTRL key, as well as the SHIFT key as well as the ENTER key simultaneously. You will be able to tell if the function has been entered properly if a pair of {} surrounds it. Don't just go ahead and add them in manually if they don't appear either. If the spreadsheet adds them then it means it recognizes the function; otherwise, you are just wasting time.

{=MMULT(B6:D7,F6:G8)}

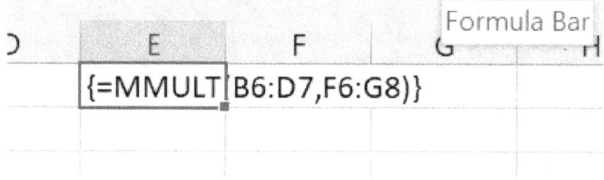

The result of the function should contain a number of rows equal to the rows in the first matrix while also containing the same number of columns as the second matrix. To determine the proper matrix product, it is important to take care to make sure the first of the two matrices contain the same number of columns as the second matrix has rows. This result will then be displayed in an area of the worksheet that you have indicated previously. It is also important to select the number of cells equal to the result or else you will only see the numbers from the resulting matrix that you initially selected.

When using this function, you may find that you come across several different types of error messages. The first is #Value! which will show up if any of the cells in the array you designated are either empty or contain something besides numbers. It may also appear if your rows and columns aren't going to align post function. If you instead see the message #N/A then it means that the cell in question is not actually going to be a part of the eventual result.

MUNIT

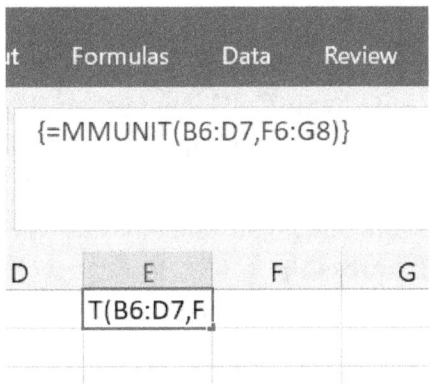

The proper format for this function is written as MUNIT (dimension). In this case, dimension represents a value that determines the actual dimensions of the matrix you are creating. The resulting number will always be greater than zero. To ensure that you correctly produce an array result for the function once you enter it into the function bar, it is critical that you first press the CTRL key, as well as the SHIFT key as well as the ENTER key simultaneously. You will be able to tell if the function has been entered properly if it a pair of {} surrounds it. Don't just go ahead and add them in manually if they don't appear either. If the spreadsheet adds them then it means it recognizes the function; otherwise, you are just wasting time.

Additionally, it is important to keep in mind that you must have first selected the appropriate number of cells to be filled with the array details as well to ensure the function works as it should. If you receive the #VAULE! then you know that the function's dimension number is either zero, empty or a non-numerical value of one type or another. This will typically result in the rest of the cells being labeled with N/A as well. It is important to select the number of cells equal to what the result is going to be or else the spreadsheet will only show the number of the matrix you selected.

MDETERM

When formatting this function, you will want to write it as MDETERM (array) in which the array is a group of values that are spread throughout any number of predetermined cells. As such, the array needs to be written as, Cell1:Cell2 with Cell1 containing the first matrix cell details and the second cell containing the matrix details of the final cell in the matrix. To ensure you correctly produce an array result for the function once you enter it into the function bar, it is critical that you first press the CTRL key, as well as the SHIFT key as well as the ENTER key simultaneously.

You will be able to tell if the function has been entered properly if a pair of {} surrounds it. Don't just go ahead and add them in manually if they don't appear either. If the spreadsheet adds them then it means it recognizes the function; otherwise, you are just wasting time. It is important to select the number of cells equal to what the result will be or else the spreadsheet will only show up the numbers from the resulting matrix that you selected.

The determinant matrix that spits out as a result of this function is computed based on the values present in the array. Assuming this is a 3/3 square matrix this can be written as A1((B2)(C3) − (B3)(C2))+A2((B3)(C2)+A2((B3)(C1) − (B1)(C3) + A3((B1)(C2) − (B2)(C1). In this case, the determinant of the matrix is the question is typically used when it comes to finding the answer to math problems with multiple potential variables. MDETERM is also useful when it comes to finding answers out to the sixteenth digit, but this can lead to issues if you are working with large matrices.

MINVERSE

When formatting this function, you will want to write it as MINVERSE (array) with the array being written as Cell1:Cell2 with Cell1 containing the first matrix cell details and the second cell containing the matrix details of the final cell in the matrix. To ensure you correctly produce an array result for the function once you enter it into the function bar, it is critical that you first press the CTRL key, as well as the SHIFT key as well as the ENTER key simultaneously.

You will be able to tell if the function has been entered properly if a pair of {} surrounds it. Don't just go ahead and add them in manually if they don't appear either. If the spreadsheet adds them then it means it recognizes the function; otherwise, you are just wasting time. It is important to select the number of cells equal to what the result will be or else the spreadsheet will only show up the numbers from the resulting matrix that you selected.

The result, in this case, will always have the same number of both rows and columns that the original square matrix had. You will always be able to multiply a matrix by the inverse matrix to create an identity matrix. Matrices that do not have inverses are called singular matrices.

Chapter 4: Macros

If you are going to be using Excel to complete the same tasks on a regular basis, then you will definitely want to look closer at macros as they allow you to automatically enter a wide variety of information that you would otherwise have to do manually. A macro is simply a group of Excel commands that are strung together with the purpose of completing a specific goal. While macros can be written using visual basic (discussed in a later chapter) but if you are just getting started and don't know how to code, then you will want to use the macro recorder instead.

The macro recorder is a useful program that will allow you to collect and store a series of steps to be issued later as a single command. The macro recorder will remember everything you do once it is turned on which means you will want to practice all of the steps manually before you press record. The macro is available from the Developer Tab which can be found under the Options menu after first selecting the File level of options. You will then need to add the Developer option to the Task Ribbon to use macros.

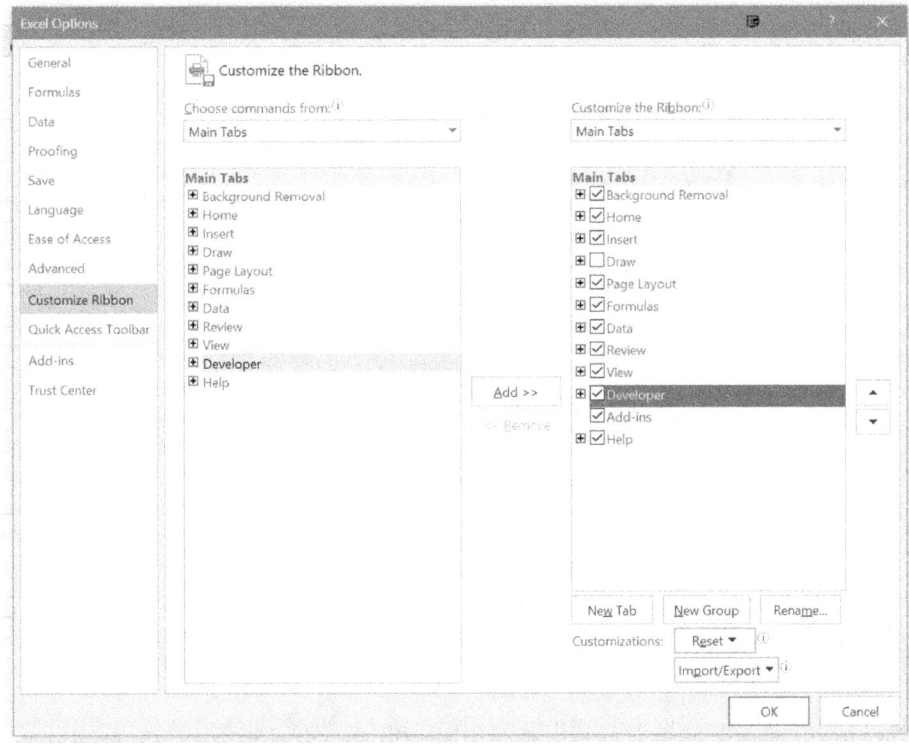

Creating a personal macro workbook

To record your own macros, you will first need to make your personal macro workbook viewable as well.

• To begin, locate the Home tab and choose the Cells group.

• Select the option for formatting and choose the option for hidden items and deselect the personal macro workbook option.

Recording a macro

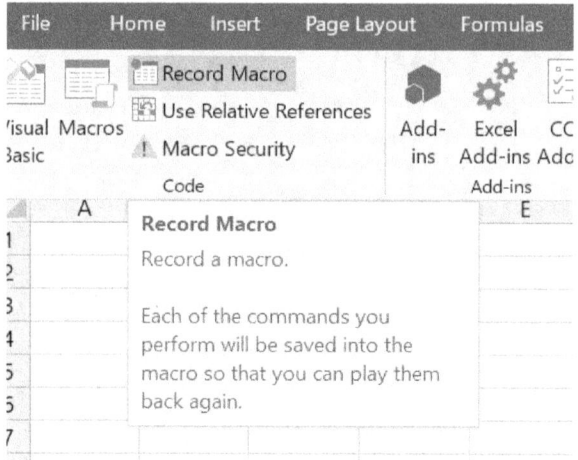

• Choose the Developer tab once you have it enabled and then select the option to Record Macros; it can be found near the Code group of options.

• You will then be presented with a name box where you will enter the name of the macro you are creating. It is important to keep in mind that your macro titles need to start with a letter, cannot include any spaces, and cannot reference any cells directly. However, the name will not be case sensitive.

• Once you have set the name of your macro, you will then be asked to assign it a keyboard shortcut. If you replace an existing shortcut with your new shortcut, then the new result will replace the old – but only in the workbook with the macro in place which is why it is better to choose unused keyboard commands for the best results.

• Next, you will need to choose where to store the macro, including the current workbook, a new workbook or your personal macro workbook – if you want it to be available in all new workbooks moving forward.

• Finally, you will be able to add a description to your macro before being given an option to confirm all the choices that you've made.

- Once all of your choices have been confirmed, you will then need to record the macro which means you will need to be prepared to do everything perfectly as all the steps you make will be recorded exactly as you do them and any references to cells you make will be recorded exactly.
- All the references are going to be specific by default, but if you want to instead make them relative, then you will need to locate the button to do so in the Developer tab and switch the option on.
- Once you select the stop option, you will not be able to record any additional keystrokes, and the macro is automatically saved to the location you requested. While you are recording, you should see the stop button at the bottom of the screen at all times.
- After you have recorded your macro, you should then be able to run it right away using the shortcut you selected. Alternately, you can bring up a list of the macros that are currently available by pressing F8. Selecting a macro from this list will run it automatically.

Give a macro to an object, graphic or control

To assign a macro to an object, graphic or control, you will first need to create the macro as normal. Once it has been created, you are then free to do the following:

- To begin, right-click on the object, graphic or control you want to transfer the macro to.
- Next, choose the option to Assign Macro from the menu that appears next before choosing the macro you wish to assign. Don't forget to confirm your decision to ensure it sticks.

Add a macro to a macro

- Start by ensuring the Developer tab is displayed as outlined above before choosing the option for Macro Security which can be found above the coding options.
- Choose the option for Setting and then choose the option to Enable All Macros. Ignore the warning that comes up but make sure you return the settings to their default state when you are done adding

macros to ensure your computer doesn't pick up malicious code along the way.

- Choose the workbook that contains the macro that you want to copy and then open the macro option from the Developer Tab.
- From the resulting list of macros that are currently available, you will want to choose the one that you want to make a copy of before selecting the Edit option. The code you will want to copy should now be available within the Visual Basic editor.
- If you want to use all of the macros, it is important that you copy the part of the code found in the End Sub and Sub Line sections.
- Once you have selected the code, you will want to open the Edit menu and copy the text which can also be done by pressing CTRL plus C.
- Next, choose the Procedure box which can be found in the code window which is where you will find the list of modules that are compatible with your chosen code. After you have chosen the right place, you will then want to choose the option to Paste.

Remove a macro

Macros can easily be deleted assuming you have the Developer tab open and ready to go using the steps outlined above. If the macro you are trying to delete is saved in the Personal Macro Workbook, then you will need to ensure the Workbook isn't currently hidden as well.

- The first thing you will need to do if you wish to delete a macro is to choose the workbook that holds the macro in question.
- Next, you will want to use the Developers tab to select the option for Macros.
- This will provide you with a list of all of the currently available macros. Clicking the X next to each will delete them. You will be given the option to confirm your choice before anything is deleted for good.

Creating a macro with VBA

- To start you will need to ensure that the developer tab is active using the steps suggested at the start of the book, you will then want to go to Macro Security.
- Choose the Settings option and then choose the option to Enable All Macros. Ignore the warning that then pops up but make sure you then return the Settings Menu and return everything to normal to ensure that your computer doesn't end up infected with malicious code.
- Once this is done, you will then want to select the option for Visual Basic from the Developers Tab and the Code group.
- This will result in the editor for VBA appearing. Choose the menu for Insert, followed by the Module option. Be aware that this will create a shortcut for all Workbooks currently active in Excel. Besides macros, class modules, userforms and regular modules can be created from this window.
- One of these windows is the Visual Basics Editor Project Window, and it will show you all of the VBA macros currently active in the open workbook.
- From there, you will need to add in the code of the macro you want to use. To ensure it works like you expect, all you need to do is to hit F5 to watch it run while still in this same window. It is important to note that the VBA features in Excel are somewhat limited which means it can't contain calls to procedures, functions (which are built in), loops, IF statements, arrays, variables or defined constants.
- Once you are finished with your macro, you will then want to select the option to Close to return to your spreadsheet via the File menu.

Chapter 5: Vertical and Horizontal Lookup

Vertical Lookup (VLOOKUP) and Horizontal Lookup (HLOOKUP) are two of the spreadsheet program's reference and lookup functions which are useful for finding a specific bit of data or range of data in a specific row or column.

VLOOKUP

To use VLOOKUP effectively, the first thing you need to do is ensure that your data is already arranged in such a way that the data you are looking for is going to always be to the right of the information you can use to find the information you need. VLOOKUP can then search columns for related information.

To use the VLOOKUP function, you will write it as VLOOKUP(lookup_value, table_array, col_index_num, [range_lookup].

	=VLOOKUP(H2,B3:E59,3,FALSE)					
C	D	E	F	G	H	
lame	Part Price	Status		Part Number	A029	
ɔump	$68.39	In stock		Part Price	$	3.43
:or	$380.73	In stock				

- In this scenario, the lookup_value is the value you will enter which indicates the value you are looking for.

- The table_array is the list of cells that will be searched and is written in the form of Cell1:Cell2 with Cell1 representing the first cell to be searched and Cell2 denoting the last cell to be searched.
- The integer entered into the col_index_num space is the column number that you want to search for the information you are looking for.
- Finally, the range_lookup function can be written as either FALSE or TRUE. If you choose true, then the search will find the closest available match based on what you entered. If you choose false, then the search will only return exact matches.

HLOOKUP

Much like VLOOKUP, HLOOKUP is used when you need to search for information related to a specific value. To use HLOOKUP successfully, you need to ensure that your data is already arranged in such a way that the data you are looking for is going to always be below the information you can use to find the information you need. HLOOKUP can then search columns for related information

To use the HLOOKUP function you will write it as HLOOKUP(lookup_value, table_array, col_index_num, [range_lookup].

- In this scenario, the lookup_value is the value you will enter which indicates the value you are looking for.
- The table_array is the list of cells that will be searched and is written in the form of Cell1:Cell2 with Cell1 representing the first cell to be searched and Cell2 denoting the last cell to be searched.
- The integer entered into the col_index_num space is the column number that you want to search for the information you are looking for.
- Finally, the range_lookup function can be written as either FALSE or TRUE. If you choose true, then the search will find the closest available match based on what you entered. If you choose false, then the search will only return exact matches.

Problems to watch out for

• If the wrong result is returned, the first thing you should do is ensure that you are sorting the column or row appropriately as either alphabetically or numerically depending on the list you are searching. If this isn't possible, then you will want to ensure range_lookup is set to false.

• If you receive an answer of N/A, then odds are you have miswritten your lookup_value. This could be because it is too small for the list table_array. If you set your range_lookup to false and there are no good results, then you will get this result as well.

• If you answer comes back as REF! then the most common reason for this is that you have entered a col_index_num variable that is larger than the number of columns available via the table_array.

• If your result returns as VALUE! then you will need to take a closer look at your table_array as it may be blank or set to a decimal.

• If the result returns as NAME? then this is because you included a word but failed to include quotations around it. If you are searching for something based on a proper name, it is vital to include the search term in quotation marks when doing so.

Tips and tricks

• For the best results, it is important that all of your references for the range_lookup end up as absolutes. If your cell references are relative, then each cell will read the reference in relation to the current location. To ensure they are set to the absolute setting you will want to press the F4 key which should bring up a menu that will determine how the current spreadsheet reads its references.

• Always write your dates out in numerical form as opposed to writing out the names of the months. If you write it out, this is likely to cause issues in the first column, especially when the table_array variable is involved. To change the existing text to date form, all you need to do is use the DATEVALUE function like so: =DATEVALUE(Cell1) and pressing the ENTER key. Cell1 can be replaced with the cell you hope to change. This will format the date as the serial number for the day, which is the number of days the date is past January 1, 1900, which is listed as serial number 1.

• If you use the asterisk and question mark properly, it can be easy to use them in conjunction with the lookup_value command. A question mark will register as a match to any character that is in the same location in the query, and an asterisk can be used as a substitute for any number of characters. For example. App?le will return results of apple, as will App*. To look up information that contains either of these characters, place a ~ in front of them.

• It is important to ensure that you do not include any extra spaces, any unnecessary quotation marks or any characters that are not going to easily print in your first column. If you do then book types of lookup will generate errors.

• You can use the clean function to delete characters that cannot be printed for one reason or another. The best time to use it is on the first column of the worksheet that you are planning on using a lookup function on. The syntax for doing so is written as CLEAN (Cell1:Cell2) with cell1 and cell2 referring to either end of the cells that will be cleaned.

• You can use the trim function to cut out spaces from a cell or group of cells that are not required. It will cut out any space that is not clearly separating two characters. This function can be written as Trim (Cell1:Cell2) with cell1 and cell2 referring to either end of the cells that will be cleaned.

Chapter 6: Pivot Tables

Pivot tables are a quick and easy way to compress and then compare large amounts of data. Excel understands how useful and necessary pivot tables are, and assuming your settings are configured properly, will not only recommend times when it seems like a pivot table is required but also create the basics for you, ensuring you are free to analyze, present and explore your data as effectively as possible.

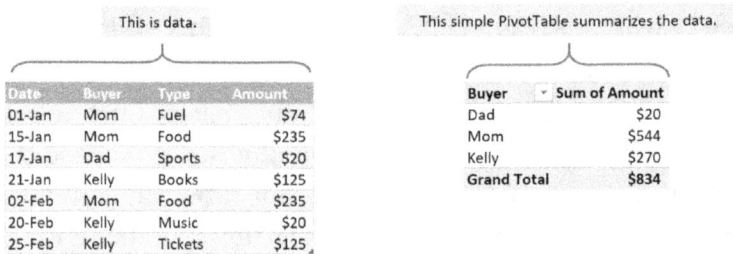

Before you can go ahead and create your own pivot table, make sure that your columns and tables are all organized with official headings and that they don't contain any blank space, hidden cells or out of place characters. Once you are ready to insert a pivot table, you will go to the Insert tab and then select the option to let Excel recommend pivot tables. This should then open a new dialog box that will suggest what pivot tables could potentially be compiled using the available data. All you need to do then is choose the one that is right for you and then provide your assent that the table should be created.

If you decide you want to delete it, then you simply select it and then hit the delete key. If this results in an error message, then you will want to ensure the full table has been selected before trying again.

Field list

Once you have created your pivot table, you will find that a pivot list is automatically generated to allow you to filter the provided data with an even greater degree of specificity. The field list can also be found under the Pivot Table Tools tab. This will provide you a list of the fields available that you can still add to the table in addition to a section of four boxes, one for values, columns, rows, and filters. You can then switch between the relevant fields as required.

Generally speaking, fields without numbers get added to rows and numerals are added to values. Meanwhile, details like dates and times are then placed in specific columns. Fields can be removed from areas using the Remove Field option.

From there, fields place in the filters area will appear in the pivot table to act as filters for the rest of the table. Fields in the columns area then appear at the top of the pivot table. While it may vary based on the specifics, you may find certain columns nestled within one another. Rows can then be found at the left of the pivot table as well as inside one another if required by their content. Values can also be found below the columns and are often summarized or show using numeric values. Multiple fields in a given area can then be sorted by simply dragging them where you want them.

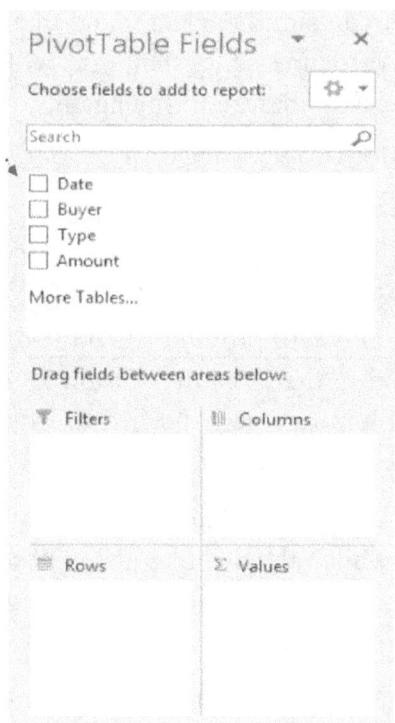

Sorting pivot tables

Pivot tables offer a wide variety of useful options for sorting, including arrows directly on the list of columns and rows. This will allow you to sort both in descending or ascending order. These arrows will then make it easier for you to access even more filters for values and labels as well as find even more options when it comes to sorting. If a column doesn't automatically include an arrow, it can still be sorted by simply choosing a cell within a row or column then right-clicking on it and choosing the Sort option.

When it comes to sorting pivot tables, you will also need to keep in mind that any data with leading spaces can negatively affect the results as they are being sorted. This means it is vital that you remove such formatting before attempting to sort the data. Additionally, you will need to keep in mind that you cannot sort text sensitive entries and you are further limited to the type of sorting you can do, which means no sorting by font color, format, cell color, and conditional types of formatting.

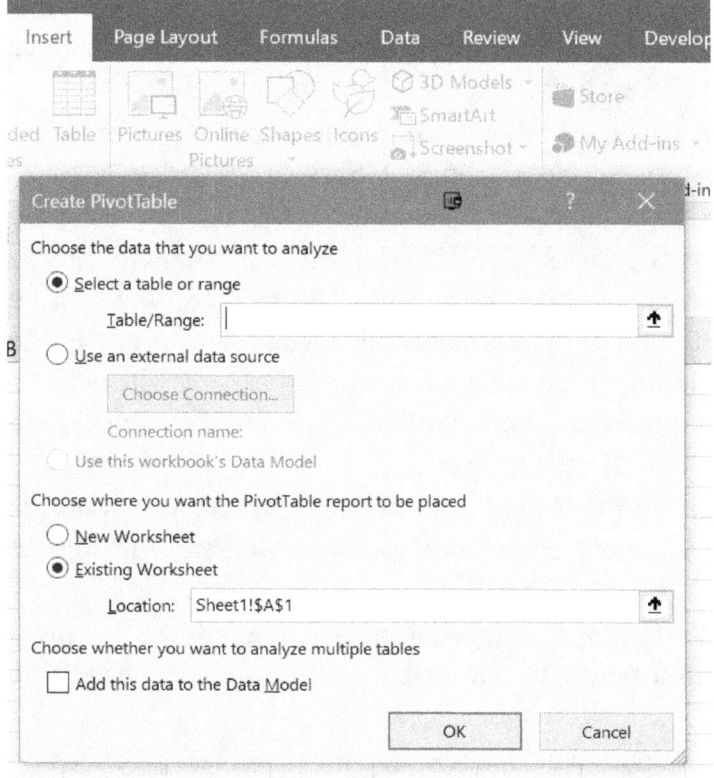

Adding external data to a pivot table

In addition to adding information that is already stored in the pivot table, you can also add external information to the pivot table as long as it is housed in either a server database, within Microsoft Accessor, or in an Online Analytical Processing Cube File.

• To start, you will want to select the worksheet you want to place the data when everything is said and done.

• Next, you will choose the Insert tab and then look for the option to generate a pivot table.

• This should result in a dialogue box with the option to determine the type of data you plan to use. Selecting this option will then allow you to select the choice to import the data from an external source.

- With this done, you will then be able to determine the type of connection that you will make which will, in turn, depend on the type of external source you are using. The next time you use this process, you will have a choice of using a connection that you have previously used successfully.
- Using the Other Sources tab will allow you to pull up information using either Analysis Services or an SQL Server.
- You can reach the access database from the tab for data, by choosing the From Access option. You will then want to choose Data Source and choose the Open option. From there you will be able to choose the type of information that you want to use in the Pivot Table. It is important to keep in mind that you will need to choose the option to create multiple tables at once if you decide to select more than one file at a time.
- With that done, you will then need to decide where you want the new pivot table to be placed, either into a new worksheet or into an existing one.
- Once you have finalized your choices, you should see the pivot table appear with a field list that contains all of your more specific instructions.
- You can also import data models into pivot tables by choosing them from the external data source choice and then selecting Choose Connection before selecting the tab for Tables.
- If you need to create a new pivot chart entirely from scratch, then the This Workbook Data Model choice will give you the basics you need to start.

Generate a single table from multiple existing tables

If you desire to place relation data into a pivot table, this can easily be accomplished by grouping the common values together. In this scenario, the field list will then show a collection of all of the table whose values you can see together. The fields from the various tables can then be moved into the pivot table as you deem necessary. To use multiple tables from the same workbook, you will first need to create a relationship between the two tables. Before getting started, it is important to keep in mind that both tables have a column which can then be mapped to one of the other columns from the table.

- When you are first starting out, you will want to ensure that this column only contains unique information and that both the tables are properly named.
- To get started, choose the Data tab and then the option for Relationships, followed by New.
- Next, choose the option that allows you to determine the base table that the others will then be linked with.
- From there, choose the option for Column Foreign and then the column that is relevant for the relationship.
- Then you will want to select the table as well as the column that you will want to connect to the initial table as well as the column in the section for Related Table/Column. Don't forget to confirm your choices before moving on.
- Generating a pivot table will then result in multiple tables being visible via the pivot table field list and the pivot table field list option.

Change the sort data of an existing pivot table

After the pivot table has been created successfully, the data that is considered its source material can be changed relatively easily.

- To start, you will want to select the pivot table that you wish to alter in order to bring up a list of pivot table specific tools.
- Underneath the Data tab, you will then want to choose the option to Analyze, followed by the option to change the source of the data.
- Next, you will need to determine the new range that you will want to use via the Table/Range box. Rather than typing all of this information in directly, you can instead simply select it on the primary worksheet. When done properly, doing so will automatically populate the pivot data with the new information.

- If the external data source has already changed beforehand, then this will likely be seen by simply selecting the option for external data sources.
- It is important to keep in mind that pivot tables that are already based on existing data models cannot be changed.
- Much as with regular tables, the pivot table can easily be refreshed by clicking on the pivot table that you wish to refresh. To bring up the tools to use with the pivot table, you will select the Data tab and then the option to Analyze, followed by the choice to Refresh; you can also use refresh all to refresh every pivot table in your workbook at the same time. You can also accomplish the same task by pressing Alt and F5 at the same time.
- When changing data in this fashion, you will want to take care to ensure the cells and columns don't reformat incorrectly by first choosing the tab for Data, and then the Analyze choice before selecting options. Select the tab labeled Layout and Format and ensure that the options for column width and cell formatting are selected.

Chapter 7: Data Models

A data model is a useful means of making the most of existing data in new and useful ways. They are also excellent at providing relational data which can then be exported to other workbooks ensuring clearly transparent tabular data results, which can then be used for things like Power View reports, charts, and pivots tables. Keep in mind that each workbook can only use one data model at a time, though multiple worksheets can use the same data model at the same time. You can locate the workbook data model under the External Data Sources option which can be found nestled in the Pivot table menu which can be found within the options for Tables.

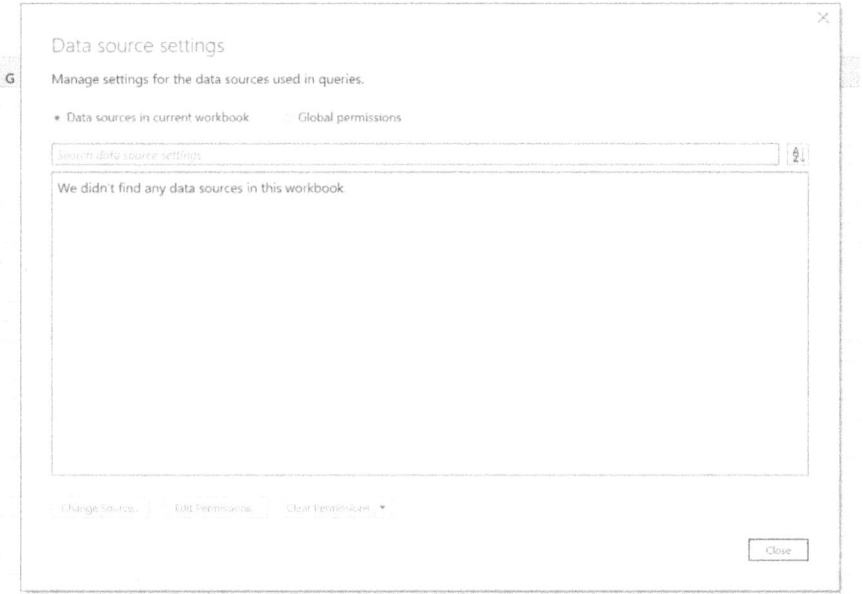

Using Excel with these models will natively only generate the standard table complete with its own field list. To get the most from these types of models, you will need to go online and download

Microsoft's Office Power Pivot add-on for your version of Excel. This add-on can be found at Support.Office.com. Once there, you simply need to search for the version of the product you are looking for and then follow the onscreen instructions to download it.

Power Pivot data is stored in its own database that allows it to access the internal search engine for queries and updates to ensure they load as quickly as possible. This data is then spread between pivot tables, pivot charts, and Power View. This data can also be remotely shared via the SharePoint server.

After you have downloaded the add-on, it will still need to be activated to ensure Excel registers it as a going concern. To enable it, follow these instructions:

- Choose the File option then Options and the option for Add-ins.

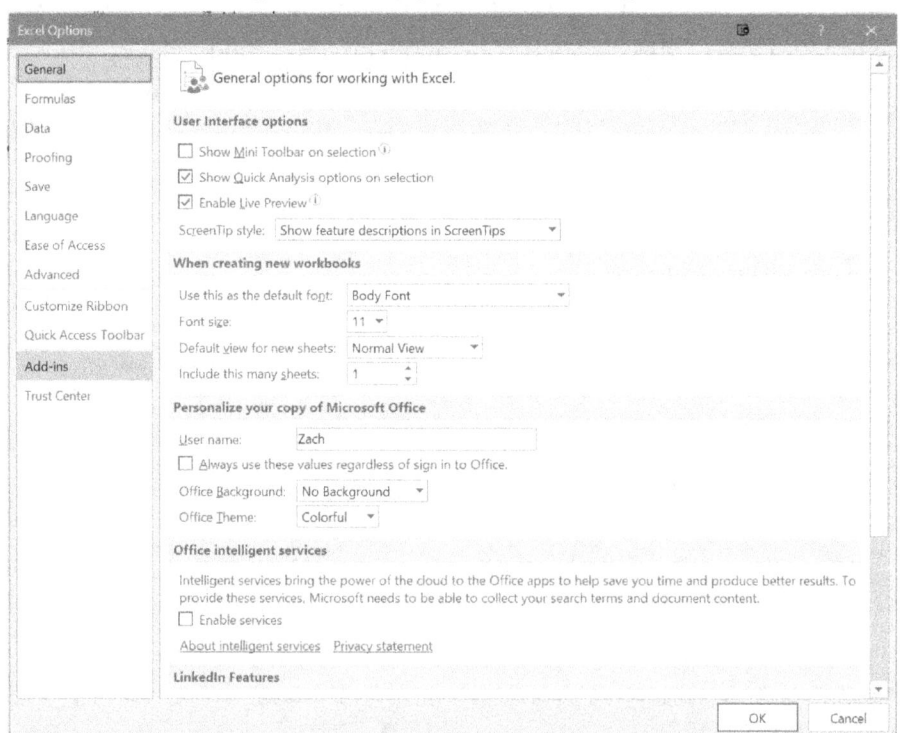

- Choose the option for Manage, then COM, then add-ons and Go.

• From there, you will want to choose the box with the Microsoft Office Power Pivot label and select the box marked OK.

• Assuming you did everything right, you will now see a new tab on the primary ribbon with the name Power Pivot.

Import relational data

If you do choose to import relational data, Excel will automatically create a data model once multiple tables have been selected, but only if you do the following:

• Choose the Data option and then the option to Get External Data. This will give you the option to choose an external source that contains the tables you want to work with.

• The resulting window will give you the option to choose the table that you want to select. As you want to choose multiple tables, click the box that lets you select multiple tables and then select your tables.

• Choose the option that makes sense for the way your data is going to be visualized and select the option to confirm. This will generate the data model that you requested, though you can still manipulate it later. This model will then be automatically updated as you manipulate the worksheet. If you rename this model afterward, then you will need to resync everything by repeating the above steps.

Keep the data model in a fixed state

As each data model is linked to a specific pivot table, changing one will affect the other. You can change this fact from any worksheet that is using the data model, though it will need to be changed for each page that is utilizing the model.

• Select the worksheet you wish to alter before choosing the option for Power Pivot and then the Power Pivot Options menu.

• At the bottom of this row of tabs, you will find a list of tables that are currently being used and what they are currently being linked to. Linked tables will have an icon next to their names.

• Choose the Linked Table option, followed by Update Mode and then choose the option for Manual. If you wish to update the data mode while it is in manual, look for the Update option which can be found under the Linked Tables menu.

Add a new data model

Once you have created a data model, it is also possible to add disparate data to it as well; this is most effective if the data you are working with is named.

• To start you will want to choose the data that you want to add to the model, or if the data is already in a named range, you will only need to select any cell that is already a part of the range.

• Next, you will want to select the Power Pivot tab from the ribbon and then choose the option for adding an additional Data Model.

• From there you will want to select the Insert tab and the option for Pivot Table. From there it is important to make sure the dialog box for adding data to the existing model has been checked.

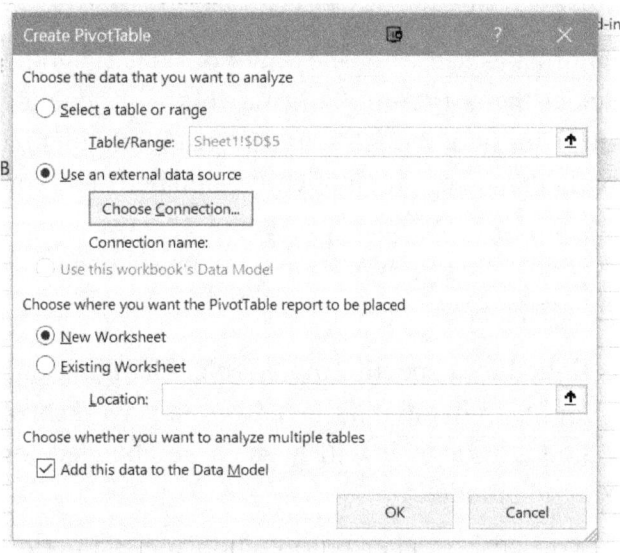

• Any additional data you add should now connect to the model as its own linked table.

Refine a data model

In the standard spreadsheet scenario, data models are typically presented as pivot tables to make it easier for folks to analyze them.

If you instead wish to interact with the data model more directly, such as by removing specific fields or tables, viewing all of the data associated with the model, adding in business logic, KPIs or hierarchies then you will find something to use the Power Pivot add-on for. Additional types of data model optimization include deciding on a field list and how it populates. To use Power Pivot:

• Choose the Power Pivot tab and then the option to Manage.

• In the new window, look for the optimization that you wish to apply to your chosen data model.

• Certain types of visualizations will only work with certain types of data.

Using Power Pivot to gather data

After you have gotten used to the interface, you will find that using Power Pivot makes it much easier to determine relational data when compared with more traditional methods. The benefits of importing data in this way also include the ability to easily remove data that doesn't actively relate to the model in question. You will also be able to rename things that you import or use otherwise predetermined terms to find data that you are interested in importing. This will also save you serious time when it comes to creating new relationships, as every table that is added to Power Pivot is going to automatically have all of its relevant relationships tagged for future use.

• To get started you will want to choose the Power Pivot tab and then the option for Home. You will then choose Get External Data and then choose the option for From Database, assuming the data you are looking for is both relational and dimensional.

• Additional sources can then be found through the use of the Suggest Related Data Option which can be found under the Data Service option which itself is found under the Home Power Pivot Tab.

- Data that is selected in this way can then either be imported straight across or filtered in a variety of different views, tables or lists of what can be imported.
- Data that is used for this model can then be refreshed from the Power Pivot tab by selecting the option for Data, followed by Connections and then Refresh All. His refresh will then look for the original data and reimport it anew. If that data isn't available, then the required connections will disappear so use this option carefully.
- Data from practically any source you can imagine can be imported. The only file type that is excepted is the option to publish server documents.

When using this method, it is important to keep in mind that OLE DB options will almost always work more quickly when it comes to scaling large amounts of data. Always look for OLE DB options when they are available.

Issues to watch out for

If you find that your Power Pivot tab stops working correctly when you open Excel, then this could be because something has gone wrong and Excel feels as though the add-on is causing the program to become unstable. This is often caused if the program crashes while the Power Pivot window is active. To restore the missing tab:

- Start by selecting the File tab, then Options and then Add-ons.
- Next, you are going to want to select the box labeled Manage followed by the option to Disable Items.
- From there you will want to select Go, then find the Microsoft Office Power Pivot option and select Enable.
- If the issue continues to occur, then you will want to close out of Excel completely.
- With that done, you will want to go to your start menu and select the option to Run before typing "regedit" into the box that pops up and hitting ENTER.

- This will open the registry editor, and within it, you will want to look for the registry key that relates to the User Setting for your version of Excel.
- Specifically, you will want to pick out the listing for PowerPivotExcelAddin, then right-click on the line item before choosing the option to Delete.
- From there you can return to the start of the Registry Editor, and choose the option for Excel Addons.
- Look for the PowerPivotExcelClientAddIn.NativeEntry.1 and right-click to delete it.
- Close the editor and reopen the spreadsheet program before following the original instructions for enabling Power Pivot.

Chapter 8: Power View

If you have already been using pivot tables as a means of creating data models, and Power Pivot as a means of manipulating data models, then Power View will complete the puzzle and give you ultimate functionality in the Excel space. It can be used as a means of presenting and visualizing data models in reports to a degree that no other Excel feature can match. Power View has the ability to take any type of data and use it to create bubble charts, pie charts, bar charts, and more. It can even break down complex tables and matrices into their component charts. Power View is only available for versions of Excel from 2013 or newer. It is also available as part of Microsoft Power BI.

When creating a Power View sheet, all you need to do is go to the Insert tab and then choose the option for Power View. Doing so should then automatically detect the currently defined data model. If your version of Excel doesn't have Power View enabled by default, then you will want to follow the steps below:

- Start by selecting File, then Options, then Customize Ribbon.
- Next, select the option for Main Tab and then select the location you want the Power View to show up.
- Choose the option to add additional commands, followed by the commands that you want to be inserted into Power View.
- Choose the options to add and then choose where you want to be able to locate the Power View option before naming the new group.
- Once you confirm your choices, you will then need to activate the add-on for Power View. To do so, you will simply need to click on

the Power View option to create on your ribbon before choosing the option to enable when given the choice.

Creating a Power View Sheet

• Creating a Power View Sheet after you have activated Power View option on the ribbon is as easy as clicking the button on the ribbon.

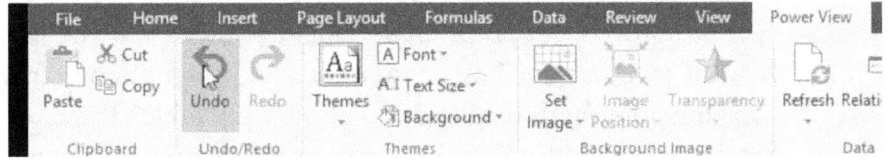

• This will then provide you with a list of options regarding tables which can be visualized. Selecting a table will provide you with a list of options that Power View has determined will provide the message of the data most clearly.

• The Design tab can be used to alter the current visualization.

Filter Power View data

Power View can also filter data based on the metadata that is provided from the data model as a baseline to facilitate the understanding of the relationships in use within the data model. The filter options can be accessed from the Filter pane and will provide additional options relating to cross-filter and slicers in addition to standard filters. This is also where the option to highlight specific portions of the data will be made available. These options can then be applied to the sum total of the current Power View sheet in addition to specific slices of the data.

You can also then apply these filters in real time by simply selecting certain portions of the data that is then being presented. To filter the data, you will then need to click on it to see what happens. For example, choosing a specific column may automatically filter the display to show all the variations on that specific type of data or highlight for additional emphasis. Pressing the CTRL key and then clicking on a value will also allow you to click on multiple values at once. Clicking on a filter instead of a value will reset the current display.

Power View and Power Pivot

If you want to use Power View with the data model, then you will need to do a few things to ensure switching from one to the other is a smooth process.

• To start, you will want to make sure you have the proper type of aggregation. The spreadsheet program defaults to Sum, so to change it, you will want to open the Power Pivot tab and then choose the option for Manage. You will then need to choose the tables that you want to change before setting your cursor on the column of your choice to gain access to the Advanced tab. You can then choose the level of aggregation that is right for you from the options menu that appears.

• Ensure you have always chosen the correct titles, images, and identifiers for all of your data model tables before you start.

Power view default

To determine the default field for all the sheets created with Power View, you will need to activate this feature. It will allow certain fields to be automatically added to Power View sheets as needed, simply by selecting a predefined table.

• To start, you will want to open the workbook which contains the data model that you want to use. You will then want to select the appropriate Power Pivot tab before selecting the Properties option.

• Select the table you wish to add a default list to.

• Choose the Advanced option, then the Default Field Set.

• Choose the Fields from the table you wish to add in automatically and then choose the Add option.

• These fields will then be added into the model in order and can be rearranged later from this screen.

• You will know you have done everything correctly when you can click on the Power View table and then have the details you need autopopulate.

Chapter 9: VBA Basics

While there is plenty you can do with Excel simply through the use of formulas, there are always going to be tasks that involve sorting or moving data around that can't be easily accomplished with this knowledge alone. In these instances, it will often be easier just to put together a simple program that will complete the task for you. This program is often known as a macro, and Excel features an easy to use means of building your own through a programming language that you can access regardless of which version of Excel you are running known as (VBA) Visual Basic for Applications.

The language operates using Visual Basic 6, a programming language that was extremely popular for a time before Microsoft created the .NET languages. Currently, VBA is the last bastion of Basic that most people are going to encounter. Even better, once you get the hang of it, you will be able to easily automate a wide variety of different functions. The language struggles when things get too complicated, but as long as you don't expect too much, you will save yourself a serious amount of time in the long run. What's more, a variation of the language is also found in other Microsoft Office products, and you will be able to adapt what you learn here with little extra effort.

It is also important to note that if you are using a newer version of Excel, then you might have a harder time accessing the VBA functions as they have been mostly buried to keep them from intimidating newer users. This means that to get started, you will need to activate the Developer Toolbar to Excel. This toolbar contains all the buttons that you will need to be a successful VBA Programmer. To add this toolbar, follow the steps below:

How to display the "Developer" tab:

1- Open Microsoft Office Excel.

2- Click on the "File" tab, the first tab that currently appears on your toolbar.

3- Now click on "Options". In Excel 2016, the "Options" button appears at the very bottom of the list.

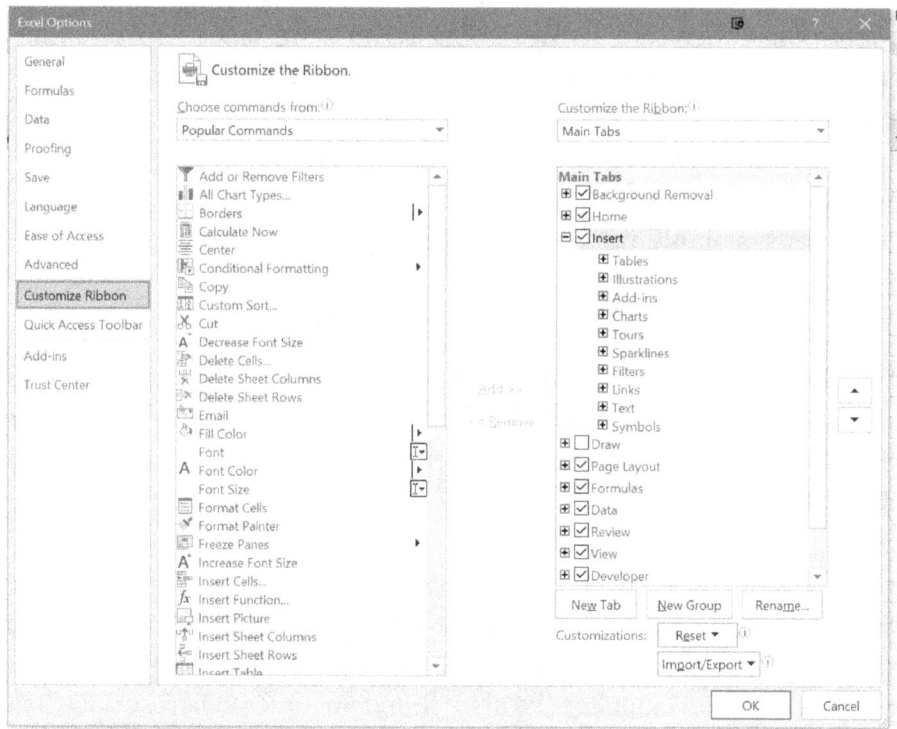

4- After clicking on this tab, a dialog box will open that contains a lot of information. Right now, keep your attention focused on the left-hand column that contains a list of more tabs. Find the tab that says "Customize Ribbon". Click that tab.

5- After clicking on this tab, the dialogue box will change to show you two columns. The one on the left says "Choose commands from" and contains a menu with all the popular commands. The column on the right says "Customize the Ribbon" and shows a menu that lists all the current tabs on your toolbar. In this menu, find the box next to "Developer"; it's near the bottom of the menu and checkbox.

6- Exit out of the dialogue box.

7- Look at your current toolbar now. It should contain the "Developer" tab near the end. With this tab installed, you are now ready to begin VBA programming!

Another task you might want to perform before beginning the lessons found here is removing the security warning. This will allow you to run customized applications without having to go through the tedious process of accepting each application one-by-one. With the security warning disabled, you will be able to run all the applications you want without any warnings popping up. If you are not using a personal computer to run these applications, you might want to keep the security warning up. The security warning might also be helpful if you want the opportunity to double check the application before it runs each time. It's up to you to choose. However, if you want to disable the security warning, follow the steps below:

How To Disable Security Warnings:

1- Click on the "Macro Security" button on your "Developer" tab. You can see it in the image above. It has the icon of a yellow triangle with an exclamation mark inside it.

2- Once you click on this button, it will bring up a dialogue box called "Trust" that opens automatically to "Macro Settings".

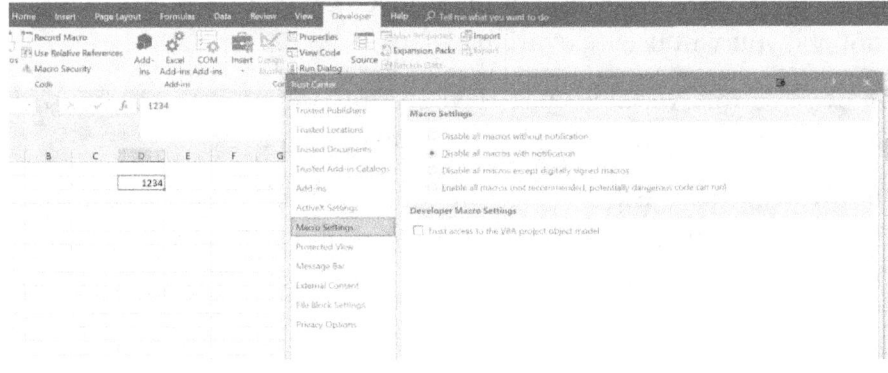

3- In the main part of the dialogue box, you will see a menu that has two parts: "Macro Settings" and "Developer Macro Settings". Focus your attention to the part that says "Developer Macro Settings".

4- Under this heading, you will see a box with the words "Trust access to the VBA project object model". By clicking this box, you will be allowing any application that you create through the VBA programmer to run automatically without a security warning. Click on this box if you want to disable the security warnings.

Now that you have found out where the "Developer" tab is located and decided how you want to handle security warnings, it's time to start programming!

VBA Programming Variables

Now that you have the basics under your belt, you are ready to try your hand at programming. We're going to start out by defining some variables. Then we will set up a program that can add, subtract, multiply and divide these variables.

When setting up a variable, there are a few options to choose from:

Integer: If you are working with whole numbers, you will most likely use this variable type. However, this variable can only store numbers from -32,768 to +32,767. If you need to work with a larger number, use the variable type Long.

Long: This variable also indicates whole numbers, but those that fall outside the range of the variable Integer.

String: If you are working with text or other characters that are not numbers, you will use this variable.

Single: Use this variable type if you are working with fractions or decimals. It will hold up to 4 bytes of data.

Double: Like the Single variable, this variable also works with fractions or decimals. However, it can hold up to 8 bytes of data, so it can be used with more precision.

To begin setting up a variable, you will need to open the Visual Basic Editor. You open this by clicking on the "Visual Basic" button on the "Developer" tab. In Excel 2016, the "Visual Basic" button is the very first button on the left. Clicking on this button will open up a separate window.

This is the window in which you will write all the programming. Let's start by setting up a simple variable.

How to set up a Variable:

1- Begin by typing "Sub" and then type "PracticeVariable". This is the title that we are going to give this set of instructions.

2- Press the "Enter" key. This will automatically set the "Sub" and "End Sub" for your first program.

3- Next type "Dim", space, "FirstNumber", "As Integer." This sets up your variable name as "FirstNumber" and defines its value as an integer.

4- Press enter and type "FirstNumber=10". Now we've defined the value of this variable as "10".

5- Now that we've set up the variable's value, let's define the variable's range. Press enter again and type a new line. First, you want to define what worksheet you want your variable to appear. Let's select Worksheet 1. Write "Worksheets(1)". Make sure "Worksheets" is plural in your code. If not, you will receive an error message.

6- In this same line of code, we are now going to define what cell we want the variable to appear in. Let's select cell A1. Write "Range("A1")". This indicates that your variable will appear in the cell A1.

7- Now, we want to indicate what variable will appear here. In the same line of code, write "Value=FirstNumber"; your entire line of code should look like this:
Worksheets(1).Range("A1").Value=FirstNumber.

8- Now that we've set up the program and have the code looking a certain way, we're ready to run it. In the Visual Basic Editor's main menu, there is a tab that says "Run". You can see this tab in the first image of the chapter. Click on this tab and then click on the first option in the pull-down menu, "Run Sub/User Form". Or you can click on the small, green side-ways triangle. That will also run the application.

9- Switch back over to your Excel Sheet by pressing the Excel icon, the first button in your Visual Basic Editor toolbar. You should see that the number 10 has appeared in cell A1.

Congratulations! You just ran your very first customized program! Now, let's make it a bit more complicated by creating a program that can add, subtract, multiply, or divide numbers for us.

How to set up a program that runs mathematical functions:

1- Open up the Visual Basic Editor and create a new code. You can continue to type the code in the same window. After "End Sub", begin typing "Sub" and add "Addition" for its name.

2- Because we are going to be running mathematical functions, we will need more than one variable. We are going to begin by defining the value of each variable. First type "Dim FirstNumber As Integer". Press enter and repeat this process for another variable called SecondNumber.

3- Next, define the numerical value of both variables. In the example code, I chose to define FirstNumber as 10 and SecondNumber as 25. You can choose any integer value you want. So far, your code should look like this:

Sub Addition()

Dim FirstNumber As Integer

Dim SecondNumber As Integer

FirstNumber = 10

SecondNumber = 25

4- Now that we've set up the values of each variable, we are ready to write the program that adds these variables together. We are also going to write a code so that one of the cells contains the word "Answers" and another cell contains the answer to 10+25.

5- In a new line, type "Worksheets(1).Range("A1").Value= "Answer". This will allow the word "Answer" to appear in cell A1.

6- Press enter and write a new line of text. It should read Worksheets(1).Range("B1").Value=FirstNumber+SecondNumber.

7- Now that we've created the program, we are ready to run it. Either click on the side-ways green arrow or the "Run" tab.

8- Go back to your Excel spreadsheet. You should see the word "Answer" in cell A1 and the number 35 in cell B1.

Congratulations! You just ran a program that performed a simple mathematical function. You can easily modify this code to perform other mathematical functions, such as subtraction, multiplication or division. For example, below is a program similar to the one we just wrote that multiplies instead of adding:

Sub Multiplication()

Dim FirstNumber As Integer

Dim SecondNumber As Integer

FirstNumber=10

SecondNumber=25

Worksheets(1).Range("A1").Value= "Answer"

Worksheets(1).Range("B1").Value=FirstNumber*SecondNumber

Recognize that, depending on what mathematical function you want to run, you will use a different symbol. The addition requires the plus sign (+), subtraction uses the minus sign (-), multiplication uses the asterisk (*), and division requires the forward slash (/).

Practice writing a few different programs that perform different mathematical functions. After you've mastered the codes needed to create these programs, you will be ready to move onto the next skill.

Conclusion

You have made it through to the end of *Excel for Beginners: Learn Excel 2016, Including an Introduction to Formulas, Functions, Graphs, Charts, Macros, Modelling, Pivot Tables, Dashboards, Reports, Statistics, Excel Power Query, and More*. This book should have been informative and provided you with all of the tools you need to achieve your goals, whatever they may be. Just because you've finished this book doesn't mean there is nothing left to learn on the topic. Expanding your horizons is the only way to find the mastery you seek.

Now, it is time to stop reading and learning and put the things you have learned into action. While some of what you have read will easily translate into action, it is important to keep in mind that you may have to try some things multiple times to get it right. If this is the case, then it is important not to get frustrated and give up. Instead, remember that using Excel is a skill, which means it will take some time to truly master. If you keep at it, however, you will find that your skill is sure to improve more and more each day until, before you know it, you are using Excel like a true expert.

Finally, if you found this book useful in any way, a review on Amazon is always appreciated!

Check out more books by Greg Shields

ACCOUNTING

THE ULTIMATE GUIDE TO ACCOUNTING FOR BEGINNERS

Learn Basic Accounting Principles

GREG SHIELDS

www.ingramcontent.com/pod-product-compliance
Lightning Source LLC
LaVergne TN
LVHW051917060526
838200LV00004B/186